1 MONTH OF
FREE
READING

at

www.ForgottenBooks.com

By purchasing this book you are eligible for one month membership to ForgottenBooks.com, giving you unlimited access to our entire collection of over 1,000,000 titles via our web site and mobile apps.

To claim your free month visit:

www.forgottenbooks.com/free908400

ISBN 978-0-266-91037-4
PIBN 10908400

This book is a reproduction of an important historical work. Forgotten Books uses
state-of-the-art technology to digitally reconstruct the work, preserving the original format
whilst repairing imperfections present in the aged copy. In rare cases, an imperfection in
the original, such as a blemish or missing page, may be replicated in our edition. We do,
however, repair the vast majority of imperfections successfully; any imperfections that
remain are intentionally left to preserve the state of such historical works.

INTRODUCTION

choice new varieties which you will find offered
for the first time in Gladioli and Dahlias.

TIME OF PLANTING

If you like to have flowers at different times,
it would be best to plant at different times up to
the 20th of June, and then you will have flowers
right along through the season.

While we exert the greatest care to have every

any re-

eplace

your flowers, tell others. If not, tell us.

Bulbs should be dug in the fall before they are
too ripe. Cut the top off close to the bulb and
leave them out side to ripen in the hot sun for
seven or eight days and then store in a cool, dry
place.

DAHLIAS

It is best to plant Dahlias in gravel and not in
rich soil. Put coal ashes in the hills where the
bulbs are. When the plants are about a foot
high put manure around the plant.

GLADIOLI

	Each	Doz.	Per 100
AMERICA.—Soft, flesh pink	$.05	$.50	$3.50
ALICE TIPLADY PRIM.—Beautiful orange saffron color	.30	3.00	
ATTRACTION.—Deep crimson with large white blotch	.10	1.00	8.00
AGUSTA.—Pale white, small rose stripes on the lower petals	.05	.50	3.50
AUTUMN QUEEN.—Beautiful cream-yellow upper petals suffused with peach blossom pink; lower petals striped carmine-red	.15	1.50	10.00
AZURE.—Beautiful bright violet with lighter markings in the center	.10	1.00	
BARON HULOT.—Rich, deep color of indigo shade	.10	1.00	
BRENCHLEYENSIS.—Vermilion-scarlet; fine variety	.05	.50	
BERTRIX.— Soft, creamy white Gladioli. Many flowers open at one time	.20	2.00	15.00
BLUE JAY.—Light blue, large white spot on the lower petals, with yellow center	.25	2.50	
BERNICE.—Light yellow, with a few red stripes that blend in very beautiful	.10	1.00	7.00
BLACK HAWK.—Beautiful dark red, with deep maroon in the center	.10	1.00	
CANDIDUM.—Snow white with flesh pink shade	.10	1.00	
CATLEYA.—Soft, lilac rose lower petals spotted white	.10	1.00	7.00

CRACKER JACK.—Dark red, throat spotted
with yellow and maroon.............. .10   1.00   7.00
CRYSTAL WHITE.—Beautiful white with
diamond shaped violet lavender mark in
the throat........................... .10   1.00   7.00
CZAR PETER.—Beautiful wine red, fine blue
spray in the throat................... .10   1.00   7.00
CHICAGO WHITE.—Pure white, with lav-
ender markings in throat.............. .10   1.00   7.00
CONSPICUOUS.—Beautiful clear light car-
dinal-red, with large white throat....... .20   2.00
CRIMSON GLOW.—A perfect scarlet of a
deep tone, flowers of immense size...... .40   4.00
CATHERINE.—Wonderful blue-gray, lower
petals a little deeper blue, with brownish
red spot............................. .40   4.00
C. M. KELWAY.—Pale shell pink, blending to
pale yellow throat which is blotched light
crimson.............................. .20   2.00   15.00

DAWN (Groff).—Beautiful salmon shading to
very light claret stain in the throat...... .20   2.00

EMPRESS OF INDIA.—Plum violet, a rich,
dark color, buds almost black.......... .10   1.00
EUROPE.—Snow white, considered the best,
clear white Gladioli.................. .20   2.00
EVELYN KIRTLAND.—Light rose, darker at
the edges, fading to shell pink at the center
with brilliant scarlet blotches on lower
petals. Very tall spikes. This Variety
wins highest approval wherever shown... .25   2.50

2

GRETCHEN ZANG.—Exquisite rose pink blending into a deep salmon blotch in lower petals. A prize winner, and especially fine for all decorative purposes.... .20   2.00

GLORY OF HOLLAND.—White, with delicate pink tint, marking in throat, large flower, well placed on long, straight spike .10   1.00

GEORGE PAUL.—Deep crimson, striped yellow, spotted purple, very large, beautiful blooms.......................... .10   1.00

GOLIATH.—Dark purple, very large flowers, an excellent variety................... .20   2.00

GIANT WHITE.—An extra large, white of great size and substance. Pure white with elegant slight markings on lower petals... .15   1.50

GOLDEN KING.—A brilliant golden yellow with intense crimson blotch in throat, giving a magnificent effect............. .10   1.00

GOLDEN WEST.—Brilliant orange, with darker mottled throat................. .10   1.00

HALLEY.—The predominating color of these flowers is delicate salmon pink with a slight roseate tinge.................... .05   .50   3.50

HERADA.—Blooms of immense size on tall, straight spike. Massive in every way. Pure mauve with deeper markings in throat................................ .20   2.00

HUBERTUS.—Extra fine lilac, flowers well placed on long stem.................. .30   3.00

INDEPENDENCE.—Rich, coral pink, briliant throat and heavy wax-like flowers.... .05   .50   3.50

IDA VAN.—Most beautiful deep salmon red, rich and brilliant color.............. .10   1.00   7.00

INTENSITY.—Light scarlet, blending lighter towards the throat................... .10   1.00

JESSIE.—Deep velvet scarlet, shaded black on edges, with light throat........... .10   1.00

JUMBO.—Deep pink, sometimes delicately flaked throats tippled deep carmine crimson.............................. .15   1.50

KLONDYKE.—Primrose yellow, with crimson blotch very early bloomer,............ .05   .50   4.00

KUNDREDI GLORY.—Beautiful cream buff with light tint of pink, crimson stripe centering each petal, ruffled........... .10   1.00

LIEBESFEUER.—Brilliant scarlet, undoubtedly one of the finest and richest colors... .20   2.00

LILY LEHMAN.—Blush white, splendid flowers irregularly set on the spike, which gives it the appearance of a lily........ .10   1.00

LILY WHITE.—An extremely fine novelty. Early, pure, white flower............. .30   3.00   15.00

L'IMMACULEE.—The best white in existence. Very tall spikes, well set with large flowers of great substance............. .15   1.50

LOVELINESS.—A beautiful cream-colored variety with darker markings. Stately spike with immense flowers........... .15   1.50

LIBERTY.—Dark red large flower and compact spike, handsome butterfly markings .20   2.00

4

MARY FENNEL.—Beautiful deep lavender flower on a tall, slender spike. Lower petals penciled with primrose yellow.... .15 1.50

MARY PICKFORD.—One of the finest creamy whites. Throat finest soft sulphur yellow...................................... .50 5.00

MASTER WIETZE.—A good dark violet with a very graceful spike.................... .10 1.00

MASTER WIEBERTUS.—Fine mauve with white mauve spotted blotch.............. .10 1.00

MEADOWVALE.—White with dainty blue throat, medium size flower, but very attractive.................................. .10 1.00

MEPHISTOPHELES.—Very large, dark red, stained with black yellow.............. .25 2.50

MISS HELEN FRANKLIN.—A new ruffled variety, pure white with slight violet markings in the throat. Tall, early, and very productive, many flowers open at one time. Winner of first prize for ruffled seedlings New York, 1917 and silver medal at Boston, 1918. Numerous awards of Merit.................................. .20 2.00 15.00

MISS LUCILLE.—An early flesh pink. Nearly all blooms open at one time............. .10 1.00

MR. MARK.—Blue with darker blotch on lower petals........................... .20 2.00

MRS. F. KING.—Light scarlet of pleasing shade. Enormous wide open flowers..... .05 .50 3.50

MRS. F. PENDLETON.—Very large, well expanded flower. Salmon pink with brilliant carmine blotch in the throat........ .10 1.00 7.00

5

MRS. WATT.—Clear crimson red, a striking American Beauty color, medium blooms, spiked tall and straight.................. .10   1.00   7.00

MRS. W. E. FRYER.—Fine, large scarlet, tall grower; wide open flower.......... .20   2.00   15.00

MYRTLE.—Pale rose, deepening on outer edge of petals. The flowers open regularly on spike.......................... .15   1.50

MRS. F. ANDERSON.—Beautiful star-shaped flower, rose pink, with dark pencil stripes .15   1.50

NIAGARA.—Beautiful creamy yellow with primrose yellow throat.................. .10   1.00   7.00

ORION.—Light rose, many flowers open at one time.............................. .10   1.00

PANAMA.—Large wax-like flowers, clear pink, large flowers.................... .10   1.00   7.00

PARLIAMENT.—Orange red, very large flowers, which are well placed on a tall, straight spike.......................... .20   2.00

PEACE.—A white flower, very large with pale violet feathering on interior petals...... .10   1.00   7.00

PINK BEAUTY.—Pale carmine with large geranium blotch on lower petals........ .10   1.00   7.00

PINK PERFECTION.—Beautiful, soft color of the carnation Enchantress. One of the largest pinks grown.................... .15   1.50   10.00

PRIDE OF GOSHEN.—A very large bloom of flesh pink. Petals waved. A stronger grower and strikingly beautiful.......... .15   1.50   10.00

PRIDE OF HILLEGOM.—The best blood red Gladioli, a most wonderful variety 20   2.00   15.00

PRINCE OF WALES.—A delicate salmon rose with a warm yellow in the throat. Early and very fine 15   1.50   10.c0

PRINCEPS.—Scarlet with white blotch 10   1.c0   7.00

PRINCEPINE.—A most wonderful variety of wine red color. Tall spikes well set with medium size flower 10   1.00   7.00

PEACOCK.—Light blue with crimson and and yellow markings 10   1.00

PRIMULINUS HYBRIDS.—Species from Victoria Falls, South Africa. The flowers are a good size and a mixture of different colors 10   1.00   7.00

ROUGE TORCH.—Large, white flower with scarlet feather on lower petals 10   1.00   7.00

RED EMPEROR.—Very large flowers of a bright scarlet color. Here we reach the summit of the scarlets unto perfection 20   2.00

SCHWABEN.—Very attractive flower, pure canary yellow; when opening shading to a soft sulphur yellow. Golden dark yellow center is blotched with brilliant brownish carmine 10   1.00   7.00

SCRIBE.—A beautiful, large, well opened flower, and an enormous spike. Color like the fine old Eugene Scribe, tinted white, freely striped carmine 15   1.50

SCARSDALE.—Tall grower, with large, pink lavender colored flowers, shaded to dark rose 10   1.00

TACONIC.—Bright pink, flecked and striped with a delicate pink, lower petals blotched a deep crimson, edged with a thin yellow stripe............................. .10   1.00

THE PEARL.—Beautiful shade of soft pink.. .15   1.50

WAR.—Deep red of brilliant color, extra large, open flowers........................ .10   1.00   7.00

WILBRINCK.—Lovely flesh pink with creamy blotch on lower petals, new and very beautiful............................. .10   1.00

WILLY WIGMAN.—Beautiful blush white, with dark carmine blotch............. .10   1.00

MELROSE MIXTURE

I have one of the best mixtures put on the market for the money. Bulbs will in digging be left on the ground and you don't know which box they belong in, so they have to go in a mixture good flowering bulbs from 1 inch up **$2.00 per 100.**

$2.25, prepaid to any part only sold by the hundred, if smaller quantity **50c doz.**

Another special offer to get a good mixture in named varieties, 20 all different prepaid to any address for **$1.00.**

15 all labeled Good Varieties prepaid to any address for **$1.00.**

Each

ADELINE KENT.—Delicate light, rose-pink; straw-colored throat with ruby dashes; are heavily ruffled from edges into center; exquisite orchid-like coloring; one of the most beautiful ruffled Gladioli in existence.................................. **$1.00**

8

AMERICAN BEAUTY.—Brilliant American Beauty color, with creamy yellow throat; one spike opening a large number of flowers at one time, forms an immense bouquet of beauty........................... 2.00

ANNA EBERIUS.—Dark, velvety purple; throat deeper shade. Fine, long, well set spikes................ .35

CAPTAIN ASHER CARTER BAKER.—Rich, velvety red with darker center...... .... .50

CELESTA DORIS.—Deep, rich, glowing red; almost solid in color.................................... .75

CHATEAU THIERRY.—Bright Cerese, red blotch, bordered by light yellow on lower petals, large, well-expanded flowers................................ .50

DR. LINCOLN COTHRAN.—Salmon-pink, striped, yellow throat; fine form and bloom............... .50

DR. F. J. V. SKIFF.—Clear, flesh-pink, light ruby center; sometimes slightly striped with rose-pink; strong, vigorous growth................................ .50

DAVID STARR JORDAN.—Immense flame-colored, with lighter speckled throat; flowers very open, like immense Amaryllis with fine, wiry, upright stems...... .50

ELIZABETH GERBERDING.—Shell pink with speckled center of ruby and yellow; heavily ruffled spikes, large and full.................................... .25

ELSE ROSE.—Cattleya pink, a blending of rose-pink shading out to white, with creamy yellow throat; orchid flowering; extra fine...................... 1.00

FRANK J. SYMMES.—Salmon-rose pink with red center, ruffled edges...................................... .50

FAIRFAX.—Solid magenta; lip of the throat light yellow with a deep magenta spot........................ .30

9

FAIRLAWN.—The largest and most beautiful dark violet purple Gladioli to date...................... 2.00

FLORA.—In color second to Golden Measure and in some respects a better variety. The best golden yellow, procurable at a reasonable price................. .50

GEORGIA.—A dark, velvety-red, it has pleased all who have seen it and one of our coming varieties........ .35

GOLDEN MEASURE.—A pure yellow, best yellow Gladioli... 3.00

HELEN TODD.—Light rose-pink with deep colored seam around the entire edge of the flower; deep scarlet center.. .25

HOMESTEAD FAVORITE.—Deep, varigated pink with many open at a time. New Seedling.............. 1.00

JACK LONDON.—Light salmon with brilliant orange flame stripes; golden yellow stripes; golden yellow throat with ruby striped center............ .... .50

LILLIAN WEBB.—Strawberry pink with light maroon velvety center; sometimes slightly striped with chocolate; stems slender, giving the appearance of a lily.. .25

LE MARSHAL FOCH.—A beautiful shade of pink, flowers twice as large as America, one of the earliest........ 1.00

LOUISE.—The showiest of all Gladioli. Clear, pure lavender, a blotch of velvet red towards the center. Resembles the orchid color...................... .75

MR. H. A. HYDE.—Snow white with faint pink under-laid.. 3.00

MRS. J. R. WALSH.—Flesh pink, flamed color center; it is a magnificent variety that should be in every collection 2.00

MRS. H. E. BOTHIN.—Flesh-salmon pink, flame scarlet center. One of the loveliest combinations in Gladioli   1.00

MRS. MARY STEARNS BURK.—Canary yellow overlaid with apricot; deep canary center; it is one of the finest yellows grown so far 1.00

MISS MAUD FAY.—Clean cáttleya pink, a light strip running through the middle of each petal . . . .   ·75

MRS. WILLARD RICHARDSON.—Deep crimson, maroon center, large, flaring flowers; an unexcelled which does not fade . . . .   ·50

MRS. WILLIAM KENT.—Light fawn to light ashes of roses; old in the throat; sometimes lightly striped with rose-pink . . . .   ·50

MRS. ALICE GOODRICH.—Beautiful white, some of the petals are daintily striped crimson, flowers stand well out from the spike . . . .   ·50

MRS. KEUR.—Fine rose-pink tinted yellow in the throat, very large and beautiful 1.00

MAJESTIC.—Delicate orange-pink, very large and beautiful, one of the best Gladioli grown . . . .   ·50

MRS. DR. NORTON.—Creamy tinted flower, light pink petals, with a beautiful yellow center . . . .   ·75

MRS. L. S. McLEOD.—Beautiful shade of lavender, with blotch of white on the lower petals (New Seedling 1921) . . . .   ·50

MARTHA FERNEKES.—Pale blue, blotched blue, violet spot in the center. An odd and beautiful blue variety which has been greatly admired by every one 1.50

MRS. THOMAS COGGER.—Deeply ruffled. Beautiful shade of pink. Awarded American Gladiolus Society Silver Medal Boston Horticultural Hall, August 1920   2.00

NORA.—Light blue, with little darker spot in throat and lower petals...................................... .50

ORANGE GLORY.—Grand orange colored, with beautiful lighter throat. Very rich and striking color...... .50

PURPLE GLORY (Kunderd).—Giant of the Glory class. Deepest velvety maroon red, with almost black blotches...................................... 2.00

PRES. C. C. MOORE.—Salmon-pink, darker throat, steel blue mottled and striped; nice, long, wiry spikes with flowers well placed.............................. .50

PRIMROSE BEAUTY.—Tall, strong. Very large primrose yellow... .20

QUEEN OF THE NIGHT.—Deep maroon, almost black; it is simply wonderful, tall, large flowers, and of velvety maroon-like burnt into the petals, and yet glossy. It certainly is a great glad............... 5 00

ROSS VALLEY.—Salmon-pink striped with ashes of roses, red peacock eye in the center............... .25

ROSEVERE.—A deep, clear, pink flower about the size of America...................................... .50

SUFFRAGETTE.—White with circle of light lilac running across each petal; creamy white throat; very delicate...................................... 1.00

SAM ANSELMO.—Pure white, slightly striped with ruby pink. Immense free flowering.................... .50

SUNSET.—Pale flesh pink, overlaid and striped with rose-pink; faint yellow throat....................... 1.50

SARAH LILLIE.—Reddish lavender; throat ruby, mottled with white.............................. .30

THOMAS T. KENT.—Rose-pink with ruby running through center of each petal; very vigorous in growth; this is one of our largest varieties.................. .50

TAMALPAIS.—Salmon orange with flame orange stripes; long, slender spikes, seedling of Mrs. Francis King, but much larger and much better in color.......... 5.00

ULRICK.—The most beautiful salmon pink grown to-day the flowers being well placed on the stalk.......... .50

VIRGINIA.—A dark, clear mauve red with a mauve striped white throat. The blooms are large and open out nearly flat.................................... 2.50

VICTORY.—Scarlet, maroon, little lighter mottled in the center; flowers very large; immense long spikes; one of our largest red........................... 2.50

WHITE GLORY (Kenderd).—Large, ruffled flower, Pure white with iris blue lines on lower petal... .35

CACTUS DAHLIAS

Each

EARL OF PEMBROKE.—Bright, rich plum color, large.. $ .30

GOLDEN GEM.—Golden yellow.................... .50

J. H. JACKSON.—The largest and best dark Cactus Dahlia to date; almost black.................... .35

KRIEMHILDE.—Delicate pink, shading to white in the center.. .30

LIBELLE.—Clear, deep, rose purple................. .30

MARJORIE CASELTON.—Rose-pink, with cream white blending at the center.......................... .35

MME. HENRI CAYEUX.—Rich pink, with a blending of white at the center............................ .35

13

MRS. C. H. BRECK.—White in the center, shading off to pale straw color, and terminating with rose-pink at the tips.. .50

PERLE De LYON.—A pure white exhibition variety of great value. Petals fringed or nicked, giving unique appearance... .35

STERN.—Bright primrose-yellow ertra............... .30

THOMAS CHALLIS.—Salmon-red or rosy-salmon...... .35

W. B. CHILDS.—Blackish maroon with purple shading one of the very best............................. .35

_____

$4.30

These twelve Cactus Dahlias sent prepaid to any address all truly labeled for............................. $3.50

PEONY FLOWERED DAHLIAS

CAECILIA.—Large, creamy-white; or undoubtedly pale lemon-yellow...................................... $ .50

HORTULANUS BUDDE.—Scarlet red............... .35

JOHN GREEN.—The coloring is exceptionally attractive and intensely brilliant, the center being a clear, golden yellow which quickly changes to fiery scarlet.. .50

LATONA.—New Holland Peony-flowered Dahlia. A buff yellow.. 1.00

MME. VAN BYSTEIN.—Rosy lilac, changing to light blue... .75

MRS. A. PLATT.—Magnificent blush-pink............ .50

MRS. BOWEN TUFTS.—Gigantic deep rosy purple, the best purple....................................... 1.00

MRS. M. W. CROWELL.—A beautiful orange yellow... .35

QUEEN WILHELMINA.—The best pure white Peony-flowered Dahlia, large............................. .35

14

ROCHESTER.—White heavily striped and splashed
  maroon.................................... .50
YELLOW TRANSPARENT.—A dwarf Dahlia, ideal for
  bedding. Lemon yellow tipped white.............. .35
ZEPPELIN.—A lovely shade of mauve............... .50

$6.65

These twelve Peony-Flowered Dahlias sent prepaid to any
  address, all truly labeled for.................... $5.00

DECORATIVE DAHLIAS

Each

CLIFFORD W. BURTON.—Bright yellow............. $ .35
FRANK A. WALKER.—A charming shade of deep lav-
  ender-pink. For garden decoration, or for cut flowers
  this variety is especially good, producing flowers in
  great abundance. Is one of the earliest to blossom... .75
JACK ROSE.—Deep crimson....................... .35
JOHN R. BALDWIN.—A beautiful salmon-red........ .35
LE GRAND MANTIOU.—A gigantic flower white, striped
  and splashed reddish-violet...................... .50
LEO XIII.—Beautiful deep, golden yellow............ 1.00
MADONNA.—Large white, with delicate blending of
  lavender pink................................. 1.00
MINA BURGLE.—Beautiful deep, glowing crimson,
  finest crimson variety in existence................. .35
MINOS.—Rich, velvety maroon, best dark, decorative.. .35
ORA DOW.—Maroon, tipped white. Very attractive... .50
PRINCESS JULIANA.—A beautiful white decorative... .50
PROGRESS.—Lavender striped and splashed crimson... .50
QUEEN MARY.—A very beautiful soft rose-pink with
  glistening silvery sheen which adds quality to its
  beauty...................................... .75

15

ROSE GEM.—A very attractive delicate pink, extra free flowering, long, stiff stem and large flower.......... 1.00

SOUV. De GUSTAV DOAZON.—This variety is the largest in existence, its gigantic flowers often measuring nine inches and over in diameter. The color is a pleasing shade of orange-red................. .35

SYLVIA.—White heavily edge pink................... .35

$8.95

These sixteen Decorative Dahlias sent prepaid to any address, all truly labeled for.................... $7.00

POMPON DAHLIAS

AMBER QUEEN.—Rich, clear amber, shaded apricot, extra free flowering; one of the very best.......... $ .20

CATHERINE.—Bright Yellow..................... .30

GOLDEN QUEEN.—The most perfect yellow pompon to date.. .30

LITTLE DOROTHY.—White occasionally striped and blotched reddish-orange........................ .30

LITTLE MARION.—Soft, salmon-pink............... .30

SAN TOY.—White, very heavily tipped carmine...... .20

$1.60

These six Pompon Dahlias sent prepaid to any address, all truly labeled, for............................ $1.25

HYBRID SHOW, COLOSSAL, AND FANCY DAHLIAS

Each

AMERICAN BEAUTY.—Gorgeous wine crimson, one of the largest and best............................ $ .50

D. M. MOORE.—Deep, velvety maroon, almost black... .35

DIAMANT.—Pure white........................... .35

16

GLADIATEUR.—Clear violet, shaded blue............ ·35
GRAND DUCHESS MARIE.—Rich buff overlaid orange;
    reverse of petals slightly edged pink.............. ·50
IMPERIAL.—Deep purplish-maroon, one of the best.... ·35
MAUD ADAMS.—The color is a pure, snowy white, very
    effectively overlaid clear, delicate pink. This won-
    derful variety is unsurpassed in quality in every
    respect, in reality a model of perfection........... ·75
MISS HELEN HOLLIS.—The largest and finest deep
    scarlet Show Dahlia in existence.................. ·75
STRADELLA.—Rich, deep purple crimson........... ·35
STORM KING.—Pure White flowers, produced freely
    upon long stems............................... ·35
VIVIAN.—White effectively edged rose violet, one of the
    largest and finest to date........................ ·50
YELLOW DUKE.—Primrose yellow................. ·50

$5.60

These twelve Hybrid Show, Colossal and Fancy Dahlias,
    sent prepaid to any address, all truly laveled, for.... $4.50

SINGLE DAHLIAS

ADVENTURE.—A pleasing shade of pinkish-crimson,
    striped and splashed maroon..................... ·30
AUBRIGHT BEAUTY.—A large, pure white variety.... ·50
BLANCHE.—A pale yellow at the base, faintly tipped
    pink, with a cast of white over the whole flower..... ·35
JOHN COWAN.—Soft crimson, shaded maroon........ ·30
MAN FRIDAY.—Deep maroon..................... ·30
PAINTED BEAUTY.—Garnet, striped deep maroon and
    tipped white. Reverse of the petals white streaked
    maroon.. ·50

17

PROSPERITY.—Light center, very heavily tipped rose-purple. 35
ROSE PINK CENTURY.—Beautiful rose-pink flowers. . . .30
ST. GEORGE.—Clear canary yellow. 50
SURPRISE.—Brilliant carmine with lemon chrome ring at center. Whole striped and splashed deep ox-blood-red. 30
THERIES.—White, striped and splashed violet. 50
VIOLETTE.—A lively shade of crimson. 30

$4.50

These twleve Single Dahlias sent prepaid to any address all truly labeled, for. $3.75

PRIZE-WINNING
PEONY DAHLIAS   Each

BILLIONAIRE.—(Stillmans 1918 novelty and listed by originator at $5 now.) This monster is one of the largest we have ever grown. A beautiful shade of golden orange. The color, size, stems and shape is quite wonderful. . . . . $ 3.50
INSULINDE.—(Peony-dec. Holland, first class certif.). Golden orange. Of greatest size and depth. Quite indescribable. Stems long and stiff as a cane. 2.25
GEISHA.—The Dahlia that made Hornsveld famous. Orange, scarlet and gold with long, irregular, curling, twisting petals. One of the most sensational, striking Dahlias grown. 75

CACTUS DAHLIAS

GOLDEN WEST.—Very, very fine for decorations and cut-flower purposes. A great seller. Gold with yellow shadings. Great size. 75

GEORGE WALTERS.—This Dahlia created many an exclamation of wonder from our visitors the past season. A very impressive Dahlia in size and beauty. Pinkish salmon with yellowish base. Blooms up to 10 inches. A prize winner...................... 1.50

GEN. PERSHING.—(New. 1919.) Curved, twisted, heavy petals. Strong grower and bloomer. Slightly creamy-white. Don't confuse with other "Pershings". Worthy of the name............... .... 1.00

KALIF.—"Majestic" describes this Dahlia in size and form. From six to eight inches in size. Long, strong stems. A kind among reds..................... 1.00

F. W. FELLOWS.—Surprisingly free for such huge flowers. Orange. Indispensable for exhibition........ ...... 1.00

PERRIOTT.—Incurved. Immense amber colored flowers with usually every petal strikingly tipped white. A stunning Dahlia and great for exhibition........ .75

TOM LUNDY.—Pa Fenton's great prize-winner that created a sensation at the Pan-Pacific Exposition. Bold crimson blooms that I believe are even more striking than the famous Kalif and I think a finer color.................................... 1.00

MAGNIFICENT.—The color must be seen to be appreciated. Oriental buff, overlaid satiny salmon. Blooms 6 to 8 inches without disbudding. Do not confuse with other Dahlias of this name................ 2.00

MRS. WAARNAR.— (Holland). A magnificent giant variety of creamy white and apple blossom pink. An acquisition of the rarest kind................ 1.00

YELLOW KING.—"Finest yellow Dahlia ever shown here", verdict of the Holland judges. Pure yellow. Curly, twisted petals and lasting a long time when cut. A great acquisition........................ 1.00

SOME WONDER PRIZE WINNING DECORATIVE DAHLIAS

MILLIONAIRE.—(Stillman's 1917 $10 novelty. Worth it). Has won prizes everywhere. A monster. Delicate lavender with faint pink cast. The depth and number of petals has never been equalled **$2.00**

KING OF THE AUTUMN.—Leading 1917 Holland novelty. Hornsveld's pride. Wins prizes everywhere. Not a monster, but a new shade of buff-yellow shaded terra-cotta. Stems up to four feet stiff like a cane. A great keeper for cut flowers 1.50

PRIDE OF CALIFORNIA.—Gold Medal, Palace Show; Silver Medal Calif. Dahlia Soc. Meda. Dahlia Soc., etc. A cross between the famous Mina Burgle and Souv Douzon with the qualities of both. Massive crimson. "The American Beauty" among Dahlias . . . 2.00

COPPER.—One of the best Dahlias ever originated in the U. S. A., 7 to 9 inches. Fluffy copper and bronze flowers 1.00

HOCKSAI.—Clear orange center. Early and free. A grand introduction and a useful cut-flower Dahlia . . . 1.50

DR. TEVIS.—A blend of copper, old-rose and old gold. Flowers grow 7 to 11 inches across, on long, vigorous stems. Fine. A Dahlia star of first magnitude 2.00

MARABILIS.—When at its best is about the largest of the Decoratives. Variously marked lemon yellow and white. Petals are twisted. A new Dahlia and great for exhibition 3.00

STRWBERRY PLANTS

FORD.—Standard variety, is a mid-season to very late. 25 plants $1.00; $3.00 per 100.

WORLD'S WONDER.—One of the very latest and largest berry grown. 25 plants $1.50; $5.00 per 100.

BUSHEL BASKET.—New variety introduced in 1920. One of the best money-makers. $1.00 per doz.

MISSIONARY.—Heads the list of all early varieties. 25 plants $1.00; $3.00 per 100.

EVERBEARING STRAWBERRIES

PROGRESSIVE.—Is the universal everbearer of the highest quality fruit. $1.00 per doz.

LUCKY BOY.—Bigger, sweeter, and more productive than any other everbearing strawberry. (New). $2.00 per doz.

Greenhouse-grown Strawberry Plants in Pots

FORD	$1.50 per doz.
WORLD WONDER	2.25 " "
BUSHEL BASKET	2.50 " "
MISSIONARY	1.50 " "

Everbearing Strawberries

PROGRESSIVE	$2.00 per doz.
LUCKY BOY	3.00 " "